From Turkish Toils

The narrative of an Armenian family's escape

Esther Mugerditchian

From Turkish Toils: The narrative of an Armenian family's escape

Copyright © 2019 Indo-European Publishing

The present edition is a reproduction of previous publication of this classic work. Minor typographical errors may have been corrected without note, however, for an authentic reading experience the spelling, punctuation, and capitalization have been retained from the original text.

ISBN: 978-1-64439-104-4

Mrs. Mugerditchtan and the children in kurdish costume

FOREWORD

The following narrative was written by the wife of Mr. Tovmas K. Mugerditchian, an Armenian pastor who became attached to the British Oriental Consular Service in 1896, and in 1904 was appointed British Vice-Consul in Diarbekir. There are many reliable witnesses who will affirm that the story of Mrs. Mugerditchian is worthy of the fullest credence. The record of the Turk is sufficiently well known; the abominations he has perpetrated in Armenia are as well authenticated as any event in modern history.

From other sources comes confirmatory evidence of the hideous crimes that have added further stains to Turkey's record in that unhappy land. Mrs. Mugerditchian and her family, dressed in Kurdish costume, succeeded in making their escape into the country held by the Russians. From

Tiflis she was able to send the whole story to her husband, who is at present seizing the British authorities in Egypt. While this small party was fleeing north-eastwards, other Armenians were making their way to Bagdad, which had just been taken by the British. Others will tell their own story, but the letter of Mr. Edmund Candler, the accredited Correspondent with the Mesopotamian forces, published in The Times of June 21st, 1917, records numerous similar instances of inhuman atrocities committed by the Turks in other parts of Armenia.

Mrs. Mugerditchian speaks of the callous behaviour of the Germans, a behaviour which can only be interpreted as connivance in crime. Mr. Candler tells us also how, at Aleppo and Ras-el-Ain, German officers stalked side by side with the spectres of famine and murder and death. "It is impolite to interfere," was the watchword. From all that this conjures up in the mind, we realise that other dragons are abroad on the earth, whose rapacities call for the united forces of civilised humanity to lay them low.

The bald statements of Mrs. Mugerditchian, A aken side by side with those that have been received in Bagdad and elsewhere, constitute a damning and unanswerable arraignment of the Turkish Government, the guilt of which must be shared by its German Allies.

Mankind must not be allowed to forget what the history of the last three years has brought to light. In a moment of anger a man may commit a crime for which he may afterwards be forgiven, but the Turk has run his mad career for centuries, leaving a trail of blood and ruin wherever he has trodden. The Germans in three years have shown that there has never been a more natural alliance than that between themselves and the Turks.

Mankind must continue to read such records as that which follows, for only thus will there be continual realisation of the evil that is in our midst.

PREFACE

To the Armenians of Kharpout and Diarbekir who have survived:

As one of those who have been saved, in an almost miraculous way, from the hell which is called Turkey, and have witnessed the atrocities committed to-day, I publish all that I have witnessed, which the Turks, in their usual lying way, attempt to keep concealed.

I write to you all that I have seen, all that I have felt, and all that the glance of the Armenian martyrs who were shot and who suffered, all that the last glance of your sisters who were violated, conveyed to me. Words fail me to describe adequately the barbarous means–burning and flaying–by which they murdered the men of intellect, Armenians of Kharpout and Diarbekir, and how they destroyed or profaned the holy places.

But those who died came to an heroic end. There were some who attempted to defend themselves with rifles of an old pattern in their hands, and to die a death of honour. Kharpout and Diarbekir, with all the district round them, have been reduced to a desert. All the inhabited villages were burnt; no Armenian males over the age of from 10 to 12 were left, the majority having been forced to adopt the faith of Islam.

In publishing this note-book, which can give only a very slight idea of the atrocities committed by the Turks, I wish to appeal to the conscience and good will of all people from Kharpout and Diarbekir living in America or elsewhere and invite them to take an interest in the fate of the orphans and widows, and to do their best in helping charitable institutions to supply financial assistance to save those who have survived. "Cherish in your hearts the feeling of vengeance for our hundreds of thousands of martyrs"– this is their call, addressed to you through an Armenian lady.

Esther Mugerditchian

FROM TURKISH TOILS

My Dear Husband–

Before Turkey had declared war you were already on foreign soil. You had taken flight from the hell that is named Turkey, in the phrase of the Russo- Armenians. One hour after you sailed from Beyrout, strict orders were received from Constantinople for your arrest; but it was too late.

Jevanian Dikran Effendi, the Government interpreter at Diarbekir, had informed us, through Professor Tenekedjian, that the British Consulate at Diarbekir had been searched, and that it was most probable that our house would be searched also; so we had taken the necessary precautions and burnt to ashes in the furnace all the English books, the pictures of the Royal Family, and all the letters bearing your signature which might arouse suspicion.

I will attempt to tell you, as plainly as possible, everything that all the Armenians and our own family have undergone, trying to summarise under various headings the events, the remembrance of which makes us afraid, even to-day.

The Armenians During the Mobilization

All classes of Armenians greatly aided the Turkish Government by putting all their physical and mental powers at their disposal and furnishing them with supplies of all kinds in abundance.

The young Armenians enlisted as soldiers and held an enviable position in the army, but the Turkish soldiers would not be reconciled with them, even with those who were serving the army with true self-sacrifice.

The following episode is worth mentioning. During some severe fighting Enver Pasha, while watching with his field-glasses, perceived four men who were fighting bravely and noted them in his pocket-book. The battle was lost. In the evening the Turkish Commander ascribed his defeat to his soldiers, but the four heroes he summoned, and when they came he was surprised to see that they were Armenians. He rewarded them by an aferin (appreciation) and by a money reward of 3 medjidies each.

The German Consul at Kharpout

The Armenians were frightened when the Capitulations were cancelled. The shopkeepers kept their shops open in fear and trembling, waiting impatiently for sunset to close them.

The German Consul, accompanied by two other German officers and guided by Mr. Ehemann, the German Missionary, visited all the vicinity of the market-place. On his visit to the Euphrates College, belonging to the American Mission, seeing the Armenian young men crowded in the hall, he was surprised for a minute. When the Director of the school approached him and said: "Do you know English?" he, after a short pause, replied, "I can speak the American language." Then, turning to the Turkish officers, he said, "I am surprised that young men of military age are still lingering in the streets. All the pupils of the school are fit for active service and the school building is quite well suited for military barracks."

Within a few days the buildings were confiscated. Mr. Riggs applied to have the living-quarters spared, but his request was refused. He at once appealed to the American Consul.

The American Consul came down from Mezre, sealed the

buildings of the school, and went back. On the day following a Turkish officer, the blood-thirsty Kiazim, unsealed the buildings. The American Consul wired the facts of the case to Constantinople, receiving the following reply: – "We can do nothing at present; the case is the same with all our schools."

The Government began to ask for bedel (money paid in lieu of military service), and demanded the use of the auditorium of the Armenian Protestants for military purposes. Mr. Riggs had willingly assigned the school buildings for that purpose. But finally the church also was confiscated and used as a hospital.

The Turkish population were very pleased with the abolition of the Capitulations, and often declared openly, "We are now an independent Government and masters in our own house, and can do whatever we like."

The Armenians were all subdued and, owing to a presentiment of impending calamity, in low spirits.

The Labour Battalion

The Armenian soldiers had all been formed, in the fields outside the city, into a so-called Labour Battalion, and were employed on the Government buildings and the construction of roads. They were properly treated at the beginning, but gradually the conditions became very severe.

It is reported that the group working in the neighbourhood of the village of Habusi, four hours distant from Kharpout, consisting of young men of from 20 to 21 years of age, was brought down to the "Red Palace" of Mezre and beaten on the way. There were among them the sons of Professor Tenekedjian, who were kept in a building starving and thirsty.

The poor fellows cried out: "Water, water," until Mr. Ehemann heard of the affair and sent some water to be given them through the windows.

On the day on which they were to be transferred to Diarbekir there were two soldiers waiting in front of the door to give four blows with a cane on the head or neck – wherever they might happen to fall – to all those who came out.

Mr. Tchatalbashian Hovhannes, accompanied by his

family, had come to see the departure of their son Nuri. The father and the mother witnessed the four blows with the club that fell on their child's head. The son, whose face was deathly pale, cried to his mother, "Could my father do nothing for me?" The mother made no reply, but fell fainting and in tears.

A young man of Huscinig reports how they were hound together in fours and surrounded by gendarmes with fixed bayonets, and how, after two hours' march, lie cut the ropes with a razor kept in his trousers, and took to flight.

Nishan, the tailor of Huseinig, reports that, after six hours' journey, orders were given by their officer commanding, Kiazim, the bloodthirsty beast, to "fall in," and immediately, at a signal given by him, to open fire on them. The orders were carried out and 1,700 young men fell dead on the ground. After a short time he shouted: "Those who are alive get up!" Being deceived by a false reprieve from the Sultan, from 120 to 130 men arose, and for the second time the poor fellows were fired on. The call was made a second time, but nobody moved from his place.

Then the gendarmes examined the dead one by one with the points of their bayonets. Those who were still alive attempted to take to flight but were shot at, only a few of them escaping alive.

The Prison Atrocities

Here are the names of the Turkish officers who showed great activity in the atrocities committed: –

Zabit Bey, the Governor of Mezre, Vilayet of Mamouret-el-Aziz;

Vahby Bey, the Officer Commanding the Army Corps;

Ferid Bey, the Officer Commanding the Regiment;

Reshid Bey, the Director of City Police;

Ali Riza Effendi, Police Commissary at Kharpout (a bloodthirsty man);

Asm Bey, the Kaimakam of Kharpout; and Shefki Bey, the Captain of Gendarmerie at Kharpout

It was on 1st May, 1915, that I saw Professor H. Bujikanian, one of the most efficient teachers in the Euphrates College, passing in custody of a body of gendarmes, some of whom were carrying his hooks. After some time I saw also Mr. Ashur Yusuf and Professor G. Soghikian. In the meantime Yervant, my son, entered breathlessly and said: "Dervartan, the Armenian pastor, Professor Tenekedjian, and some other men of high standing have been or are being arrested, and the whole city will be searched." Let me tell you that Ali Riza Effendi acted as the executioner throughout those terrible days.

I gathered round me all my children and we began to pray together for those imprisoned and for the whole Armenian nation. No member of the male sex was to be seen in the streets; most were in prison. The police authorities often declared that they would be released at once, hut they remained in the prison for a long time.

They were all right for the first three weeks, and were allowed to communicate from the windows by signals and to send greetings to their relations. As the adults were afraid of being seen in the streets, our little Arsen acted as means of communication for them.

Later on came the days of terror; Professor Tenekedjian, Professor Bujikanian, and Dervartan the pastor were tortured and maltreated. They hung them head downwards, plucked the hair of their heads and moustaches, and pinched their bodies with pincers, under the pretence of endeavouring to make them disclose some secrets. The prisoners cried in vain for help.

Here are the particulars of the tortures which Professor Tenekedjian underwent. Professor Soghigian declared that his moustache and beard were so pitilessly plucked out that when he was shown to him he could not recognise him, notwithstanding his friendship of over thirty years. There was no limit to the Hogging he endured. They crushed his hands and feet in the press, ami pulkd out his nails with pincers; they pierced his face with needles, and put salt on the wounds; they forced him to take eggs out of boiling water and put them under his armpits until they cooled. They hung him head downwards from the roof, beating him all day long; they forced him to stand up for eight days in a drain, and they hung him head downwards for three hours in a water-closet.

The people outside the prisons knew of what was going on only from the cries and moans which came through the walls; while the food supplied for the imprisoned persons was usually consumed by the warders, the poor prisoners being left to starve.

An attempt was made, with threats, to induce Professor Tenekedjian to sign a document which read as follows: "The whole Armenian Nation, from the children of five years to the aged of seventy-five, consists of revolutionists, and the Armenians plotted secretly to massacre the Turkish males by rifles and the females by means of razors." All threats were in vain, so they sent for some scavengers and ordered them to urinate into the professor's mouth; then they put a red-hot copper vase on his head, burning his scalp and hair.

Professor Bujikanian was exposed to the same tortures. After the usual torments they pulled off his nails and seared the wounds with hot irons until he went mad. But when they asked him: "Where are the rifles?" and in reply he said, "The rifles are in my head," they cruelly pressed his head under the press. When his wife took his blood-stained shirt to the German missionary, Mr. Ehemann, he only replied: "I can do nothing."

Mardiros Muradian was exposed to the same tortures by the Turks. First of all he was given 1,600 lashes; then they put out his eyes, and in this miserable condition led him round the city, and took him again to the prison, where Riza, the Police Commissary, kicked him to death. The day following they sent to his wife the blood-stained carpet on which he was killed. Orders were given to bury him at three o'clock in the morning without a coffin and face downwards, to prevent the pastor seeing his disfigured features. During the burial the pastor saw clearly that his face had been burnt by sulphuric acid.

The nails of Professor Lulejian were pulled off, and his fingers were burnt with a hot iron; he was forced to walk on iron nails, and his buttocks were cut with a razor.

Those Who Died of the Flogging

Armenag Tervizian and Garabed Tashdjian were so cruelly flogged that their bodies were all swollen; they were taken to the Turkish hospital in a pitiful condition, and a pretence of performing an operation on them was made. They died within two days.

Mrs. G. Tashdjian, who was pregnant, was hung up by her arms and beaten for four or five hours to make her tell where the rifles were kept.

Shekvi Bey, the Captain of Gendarmery, strangled fifteen young men in their beds, binding them to each other.

It was a heartrending scene when they took Professor M. Vorperian to prison with a night-shirt on, at midnight, while his wife and children made pitiful lament; and his old mother-in-law, weeping and lifting up her arms, cried aloud, "Come down, Oh God Who hast created us, come down !" The policemen took not the least notice of their cries.

After a while the Reverend V. A. was taken to the prison. Hadji Hagop Fermanian was flogged in front of them until he fainted; then water was sprinkled on his face to rouse him, when they continued the flogging even more cruelly.

13

This they repeated three times in order to make him disclose the place where the rifles were kept. At the same time they threatened the other people, saying: 'Tf you do not bring and hand over the rifles of the Armenians by to-morrow, you will suffer worse torture than this," and they pointed to the tortured body of Fermanian.

Professor Vorperian was delirious the whole ni, ht, and on the day following he was taken to the American Hospital at Mezre in a car, accompanied by two policemen.

The Reverend V. A., after remaining in the prison for eight days, became very ill.

They showed Professor Tenekedjian to the people in his altered condition, saying: "Here is your enemy." Not. satisfied with the ordinary tortures, they whipped him on the hands and burnt his hands and feet, and Hayed him alive.

False information, signed by themselves, was sent every day to Constantinople, with pretended revelations about the revolutionists, and pictures of so-called rifles (the use of which is forbidden) were taken, all of which were intended to incriminate the Armenians. To give a clear idea of the information sent to Constantinople it is sufficient to mention the following. Mardiros Muradian, who had been driven mad through the severity of the flogging, was taken to his house to show the place where the rifles were kept.

The wretched man, who had no rifle at all, pointed out certain places as the "places where the rifles were kept." They dug the places out and found absolutely nothing, but they reported to Constantinople as though a great quantity of arms had been found.

Mrs. Esther Mugerditchtan

Collecting the Rifles

The people, terrified by the atrocities committed on well-known persons, had cleared their houses of everything which could possibly arouse suspicion. We had burnt even the school textbooks. Any book on chemistry, etc., might be sufficient reason for denouncing the owner as a student of bomb-making. A town crier went round for days and days announcing that every Armenian was obliged to hand over the rifles that he had to the Government. Men were imprisoned one after the other on a charge of possessing rifles. The licensed gunsmiths were all thrown into gaol and heavily fined Many of them, owing to the tortures they underwent, sent to their houses to tell their families to buy rifles from the neighbourhood and hand them over to the Government, hoping to save themselves in this way.

The houses were searched; the suspected places were dug up to a depth of three to six feet; the walls were demolished and the floors were pulled up under the false pretext of finding rifles. Everything that met their eyes during the search was carried off.

The Government was not satisfied with the things collected. Some of the Turkish officers and Mr. Ehemann often declared on oath that all the imprisoned people would be released, providing that all the rifles were handed over to the Government. Mr. Ehemann, taking an oath in the name of Christianity, gave an undertaking that no harm would be done to any person. So the sporting guns too were handed over to the Government.

Once rumours arose that the imprisoned people were to be released, but the day following it was said that 70 bombs were discovered in Mezre. The people were terrified.

Exile

There were rumours on June 20th, 1915, that all the imprisoned people would be transferred to Mezre in order to be interrogated by a German Court and that they were to be released if they proved to be innocent. It was obvious that the Germans had decided to exterminate the Armenians in their country. It was rumoured that the German Consul in Erzeroum was the first to kidnap a beautiful Armenian girl. The Germans behaved everywhere as cruelly as the Turks towards us Armenians.

The relatives of the imprisoned people petitioned to be granted permission to see their loved ones for the last time. It is impossible to describe here this interview – their last. They were not allowed to exchange a word; the tears were running down their faces, and all were reduced to the likeness of skeletons. A father, Malyemezian, was allowed to kiss his child of nine years old, to whom he said in an audible voice: "My dear, they tortured us like Jesus." The same night they were all transferred to Mezre.

On Wednesday, June 23rd, at midday I returned in terror to my house from the neighbours, gathered my children round me and prayed, having no other means of consolation. Araksi, my girl, said: "Mother, your tears and pale face denote that the Armenians are living through critical hours." In truth, a terrible massacre was hanging over us.

Before the exile the prisoners were searched, and everything found on them was taken as a precaution, leaving nothing for the Kurds. Those who were badly flogged were sent off first of all, in carts, but the carts returned empty within half an hour.

The daytime on Thursday was as silent as the night; nobody was to be seen in the streets but the young boys bringing home the blood-stained clothes of their relations.

On June 24th it was announced by a town crier that it was the women and girls' turn to be exiled. The inhabitants of Mczre had to leave on July 1st, 2nd, and 3rd in the direction of the Arabian deserts. A small caravan was sent off on July 1st, and on the 3rd 1,000 families of richer class. Heaven and earth were full of their cries and moans. It was said that they were to be transferred under guard and in security.

On July 4th all the Armenian inhabitants at Huseinig, without exception, were sent off, but at a little distance from the city they separated the males from the females and killed them with unheard-of tortures.

The good-looking women and girls were ravished by the Kaimakam, the Major, and some other Turkish officers, while the ugly ones were exiled towards Deir-el- Zûr.

On July 5th the town crier announced to the people that they were to be ready to start for Arabia. Few of the men were sorry, hoping by this means to be saved from Turkish atrocities. So all who were hidden came out of their hiding-places and all were sent to exile, even those of 15 years of age. The same evening the Turks announced with joy that 100,000 of the enemy had been massacred. "We have massacred our enemies; our enemies have been massacred." We saw Armenian women wandering about and climbing up the hill, with a parcel of bread, crying: "Taken away, taken away!" These were maddened mothers and women trying to get near to the caravans, which were surrounded by gendarmes. The caravans consisted of people who were marched along in rows of four. All were killed the same day.

On July 7th even the old and sick were not spared; they were beaten and mauled about the streets. Among them were Menneyan Hagop Agha and Kalnean Sarkis Agha. After a while the town crier announced again that there was nothing to be afraid of; everything was over, so those who were hidden came out of their hiding-places, but they were soon taken away and killed.

While the inhabitants of Kharpout were getting ready, some of those exiled from Erzinjan and Erzeroum arrived and urged the people not to move at any cost. The people were aware now of the atrocities committed during the journey, so on one occasion they rushed to the Government house, shouting: "Massacre us here and not in exile."

The Government issued a document called a vesika, the bearer of which was permitted to stay in the town. This permit was for a short time only and the vesika could only be procured by means of bribes. The following were allowed to remain in the city: –

1. Those who had young children.
2. Boys under thirteen years of age.
3. Artisans and their families.
4. Pregnant women whose day of delivery was very near.
5. Families of medical officers.

Those who had obtained the vesika were not allowed to appear at all; otherwise exile and death was likely to be their fate.

The American missionaries put their buildings at the disposal of the Armenians to keep their effects in, but the Government prevented this by placing the building under guard, to avoid anything going in or coming out.

Mr. Riggs, Dr. Parmely, and Miss Harley wanted to accompany the people in their exile, but were not allowed. Dr. Parmely went from house to house distributing drugs to be used during the journey. They did whatever they could. Mrs. Henry acted truly like an angel. Some women came to ask my opinion about accepting the faith of Islam. I am glad to announce that, nobody did so, all preferring to die as Christians.

The Exile of Our Family

While these things were happening and indescribable cruelties and severities were being practised, your friend V. sent to assure us that there was no danger at all; but I did not pay the least attention, presuming that a Turk was always a Turk. Having ascertained everything myself, I applied to V., informing him that I did not wish to go into exile, and at his suggestion and with the help of your friends V. and M., succeeded in getting a vesika.

Some days later thirteen men of the gendarmery made the following proclamation through a town crier: "Everybody is to open his house door and let us sell all his effects and property. We shall to-morrow seal all the houses and nobody will be allowed to take anything out of. them." The doors were knocked at one by one; we opened our door in our turn and everything in the house was sold at a ridiculously low price. Later on Turkish women rushed in to ransack our property.

One day they wrote on our door: "Exile." When our vesika was shown to them by my young boy, they replied: "The Sultan lias given more recent orders." Nothing was left in our house, so that our Turkish friend said: "Now Turkish people will not be interested in you."

In the Costumes of Kurdistan

Mrs. A., Mrs. Derghazarian, and Mrs. Filibosian called me in in great haste. The mother-in-law of the latter had told them that the men of Kurdistan were of the Syriac Church. So they had appealed to this Church to have themselves accepted as members. Only the family of Filibosian were approved as Syriacs, while the others were refused. I told V. and K. that, when the Armenians were massacred twenty years ago, the Turks at Mezre protected the Armenians there and in the end they themselves were benefited by them. The Kaimakam had lightened the tortures, and the exile of the inhabitants of Kharpout was delayed for fifteen days, when the notice: "Exile," was put on our door.

Accompanied by Mrs. A. and our Arsen, I went to the American Hospital at Mezre, and from there applied to the Kaimakam, asking him if there was a means of getting free. "It is necessary to adopt the religion of Islam," replied he proudly. Hut when I refused his proposal, saying that it was impossible for me to change my religion like a shirt, and that I could not deceive God, his wife, moved by a feeling of pity, asked her husband to propose something else to us. The Kaimakam demanded a sum of £100. I returned sorrowfully to the hospital, because for all our property, worth £400 or £500, we had received only £15, and we had already bought a donkey for the journey.

Dr. Atkinson admitted my girl to the hospital as a nurse, and at my request Yervant was admitted as a druggist, and Zenop as an orderly. I myself hastened back to Kharpout. It was necessary to send them to Mezre before dark. Our departure was as sorrowful as death. We were all weeping.

At the last moment the idea occurred to me to try to satisfy the Kaimakam with a sum of £50 if possible. I asked Dr. Atkinson to advance the said sum and he would get it back from you. As soon as I received the money from the kind-hearted doctor, I called immediately on the Kaimakam. He took it with satisfaction shining in his eyes and said that he would feign ignorance of our presence, and that we must hide ourselves in a place away from the city.

Our joy was unbounded. We had intended to go with Arsen to the hospital to hide ourselves there. We got the indispensable things and disguised ourselves as much as possible. We had never expected that our situation would end so favourably. We were to spend that night, too, all near one another.

Before our flight from Kharpout it was necessary to hide all our photos. We placed them under the ground floor.

Yervant and Zenop were all the time concealed in the house, hiding themselves by day, in a hole three to six feet deep, only coming out by night to breathe fresh air. Araksi and I had to manage the household affairs.

26

By means of a dirty tarbusli or a torn zabun (long Turkish dress) it was possible to assume the appearance of a typical Kurdish child. Yervant put on a short zabun, as suggested by V., to prevent him being taken for an older person.

Arsen was altogether disguised. All his exertions manifested his endeavour to save a whole family, as he went to the Kaimakam or the police, applied to the Vali, etc. Your child acted your part so skilfully that he filled the place you left.

Fifteen Days in the Hospital

On Saturday, July 16th, two days after our removal to the hospital, I called, with my two girls and Arsen, at my sister's to see her husband the Reverend A. E., who was living in the German Girls' Orphanage under the care of a German-Swiss missionary (Tante Katarina) to avoid being sent into exile. The Reverend A. E. was very glad of this arrangement, but, alas! it was for a short time only. Mr. Ehemann, the German missionary? four days after our arrival, sent to say that "he could not undertake the responsibility in case a search was made for Mrs. Esther and her six children by the Government." So we were compelled to leave. The Reverend Asadur wept like a child at our departure.

Dr. Atkinson cordially welcomed us. Our little children were admitted as playmates for his little ones. The hospital was soon crowded with Armenian refugees, women and girls. The doctor kindly admitted the crowd, which totalled 200 persons. There were besides about 200 wounded Turkish soldiers. The doctor appointed the Reverend A. and me as overseers to these 200 persons, who remained there as hospital orderlies.

Nobody dared to leave the hospital for fear of being seen. Zenop was working in the cellar with the doctor's child;

Yervant as the assistant to the druggist; Arsen was employed in bringing water on a donkey, so we all were busy and had something to do. On Sunday, July 18th, the exiles from the upper town of Kharpout passed along the road north of the hospital. Many watched their parents go by for the last time, in spite of strict orders from the doctor forbidding all to watch them.

The American nurses, who watched the procession from close at hand, told us that the women had veiled their faces and put on shalvars. Many were on foot, and some, having no other means of transport, were on donkeys. The young children stood still on the road, weeping and crying: "Mother, we are tired"; but the stern faces of the gendarmes and the blows of their whips compelled them to go on until they fainted and fell down. The lady teachers of the Euphrates College had veiled their faces. When asked by the nurses who they were, two of them replied that they were Zaruhi Benneyan and Mariam Tashdjian. During the week the exiles from the other districts of Kharpout passed along the same road.

The attention of the Turks was then directed towards the Armenians in the hospital. In order to protect the lives of the young men there, Dr. Atkinson assigned them a large room in his house. Later the hospital was surrounded. Miss Campbell, at my request, gave me the key of her dormitory and ordered us all to be transferred there until the arrival of the news which she was expecting from the American

Consul. I was looking after my children when Henry entered breathlessly, saying that Yervant and Arsen were hidden in a very safe place and that we had nothing to do but to go to the place assigned to us.

It was late at night when Miss Campbell came in and told us to get ready to go to the American Consulate. Within ten minutes Dr. and Mrs. Atkinson, my children and I, and Miss Campbell were ready to go, accompanied by a Turkish sergeant-major belonging to the hospital.

On the way the sentries stopped us more than once, but the Turkish sergeant-major whispered to them, and they let us pass. We passed the night on a carpet, seven of us under one bed-cover. In the morning, when we opened the windows, the wind blew the smell of tincorpses towards us and made us feel quite sick. Our three children and Professor Luledjian remained hidden by day in a room in the upper story and could come down to breathe some fresh air only by night.

The professor told me how he and his family were saved from the massacre and exile. Miss Campbell was Scotch, but the Government recognised her as an American. She declared to him that she loved his brother Levon and so she would try and save the whole family. "Please allow me," she said, "to become engaged to Levon, not with the idea of getting married, but to have grounds for protecting you by pretending that he is my betrothed. I cannot, though I love bun, force Levon to marry me; I am ten years older than he. I want to make him my betrothed so as to save him. He can afterwards marry anyone lie likes." Tin's lady, in truth, saved the whole family, accommodating them in her own or her lady friends' houses. Later, an opportunity presented itself and they fled to Dersim.

Let me tell you a fact that should be mentioned here. Professor Soghigian had been flogged in the prison and transferred to the military hospital three days before the exile. After he had somewhat recovered he was sent back to his family, but his experiences had left their mark and he ultimately died, though a natural death.

A few days after our taking refuge in the American Consulate rumours were circulated that 200 Armenians had taken refuge there and that the Consul had been placed in a very difficult position. The Capitulations had been annulled and his attitude was uncertain. During this time Dr. Atkinson proposed to our elder girl that she should work in the hospital (she sometimes played the piano for the patients). The same day Yervant also was admitted as druggist. The doctor took Alice and Armine to his house, made them playmates for his little ones, and even taught them English.

The American Consul was troubled by the large size of our family. So Arsen passed a month in the Swiss- German Orphanage. Zenop and I remained in the Consulate and so we were separated from each other for twenty-three days, but we were tired of idleness. Zenop was appointed later on hospital orderly, and I acted as cook in the kitchen of the hospital. Arsen could not bear the life in the orphanage, so we took him to the hospital, where he was employed as a carpenter's apprentice. We were all together now, and devoted whole-heartedly to our work, being the only family in the Kharpout province which had been saved from exile and massacre.

In the human slaughter-house (Kassabhane) of Kharpout the Armenians brought down from Erzeroum and Erzinjian were pitilessly killed with axes, spades, knives, and bayonets. The military were musters of everything. The Kavass of the American Consul told the following story of what he had witnessed one day during a walk: –

"To the south of Mezre, one to one and a half hours' walk away, very many mothers had been cut to pieces and lay swimming in their blood; wounded children were screaming; little babies of eight to nine months old hung on the breasts of their mothers; hundreds of corpses were scattered everywhere, from among which came moans and cries of agony, some calling: 'Water! water!' Mr. Picha[?], an Austrian, the Director of the Ottoman Bank, overcome by the scene, wept like a child and galloped away. Mr. Davies also accompanied us."

On one occasion a child of fifteen years old, Hrand

Mughalian, was brought to the hospital with five swordwounds in his hand and two bullet wounds in his loins. The kind-hearted doctor attended him and restored him to consciousness. When he had to some extent recovered he told the following story: –

"Four hours away from Kharpout they led the caravan of exiles, which consisted entirely of members of the Shagalian and Mughalian families, down into a valley and there fired on and bayoneted them. I fainted and fell down. They examined the corpses to ascertain if they were all dead. A few hours later, when I had recovered consciousness, I fled in terror from the valley. My feet were not wounded but they were not strongenough to carry me. A little farther on I met an old man who allowed me to ride on his donkey and brought me here to the door of the hospital and told me to go in."

Some of the Armenians who had remained in the German Orphanage asked Mr. Ehemann to send a telegram to the Missionaries in Urfa to find out whether their relatives had arrived there. Here is the reply given to the telegram: – "The exiles have not arrived here, and will not. arrive either. That is the fate that was intended for them."

More than ten persons, who were wounded during the exile, were brought to the hospital, among them a child seven years old, shot in the head, with the bullet still in his skull. A carpenter from Habusi named Brother Marsub, who had received forty-three bayonet wounds, was hardly able to drag himself to the hospital. The doctor healed him. This is what Brother Marsub related: –

"They bound us and took us to a place far from the village, where our graves had been dug. We had no means of defending ourselves. The gendarmes bayoneted us one by one and pushed us into the graves. After several blows I fainted, and, when I recovered consciousness, found myself covered with earth." The Turks established an orphanage for the young children in the village, but later, thinking it unnecessary to feed them, put them into carts, took them off and killed them with swords and axes.

Itchme was also subjected to a massacre. The males of Habusi were killed in a building near the church of Itchnie after being tortured for ten days. Mr. Aramsaradjian was one of them. The village of Morenig, where Turkish deserters were hidden, was burnt, and it was said that they were Armenian Fedai (revolutionaries), and those who attempted to flee from the fire were shot. After a short examination it was found that they were Turks. We could see the burning villages clearly from the windows of the hospital.

Mr. Setrak Zulumian had volunteered to try and get through to Russia with his two friends and tell them of the miserable state of the Armenians, but the Turkish soldiers killed them near Habusi. All the holy places were burnt and ruined.

Harutun of Palu, a young boy twelve years old, related that his friends of the same age were taken away, tied together in fours, and killed by having their heads crushed with stones.

The Second Raid on the Hospital

The Reverend A., his wife and his four children had taken refuge in the hospital. At first my elder girl was appointed as assistant to the nurses, but when she was expert enough a large ward, where there were two senior officers, three captains and three kolaghasis, all of Turkish nationality, was placed under her charge. The Turkish sergeant considered the pastor Dervartan and me as obstacles to the realization of his immoral inclinations.

One day at dinner-time all the nurses rushed out to see the policemen who were walking on the balcony- My elder girl saw that I, Arsen, and many Armenians had been arrested and were being taken to the prison; bowever, she kept her presence of mind. The sergeant had betrayed us and the hospital was cleared out. An Arab officer hid Zenop under his bedstead. Yervant was in the pharmacy.

The Turkish sick were very pleased at the arrest of the Armenians. A Turkish officer, who had ravished Professor Vorperian's girl, declared: "We have proclaimed to the world that the Armenians have revolted, that a large quantity of bombs and grenades was discovered, etc., only in order to justify our actions. Our purpose has been to exterminate the Armenians since the day when Boghos Pasha Nubar introduced the Armenian question to the

European Governments. The abolition of the Capitulations was a blessing to us for the realisation of our object. If our purpose had been to punish only the offenders, the people would have been spared." Some other officers declared: "The Russians also do not like Armenians, even though they assist them," and so on.

A few days later we were released, with the workers in the hospital. It was the first time that Armenian prisoners had been released. During these days the doctor called me and gave me your letter. Our joy was unbounded. I asked him to put a large room at our disposal. There we celebrated Yervant's birthday and the receipt of your letter. The meeting was presided over by the doctor. Yervant played the violin; Arsen accompanied him on the flute. The nurses asked the doctor to allow Araksi to sing the "Grung Tchan" ("My Lovely Crane"), by Gomidas Vartabed, and she sang the song in a thrilling voice.

> Sing, thou crane, sing,
> While the spring is still here;
> The heart of the Armenian exile
> Is bleeding.
> Lovely crane, lovely crane, it is spring,
> But, Oh! my heart is bleeding!

All the Armenians in the room wept, feeling that they were really orphans now.

The next day, as we were allowed to live in freedom, I hired a house, where Arsen, Alice, Armine, and I lived.

Mr. Riggs and Mr. Ehemann applied to the Vali to have a telegram sent asking for pardon for the remnant of the Armenians. The Vali said: "There remains only one means of executing your request. I can send a telegram saying that the offenders have gone. Those that remain are innocent; imperial pardon." On this reply they did not persist in their request, foreseeing that the result would not do good.

My Second Imprisonment

On November 4th the day was so bright that the majority of the nurses and orderlies went out for a walk. I was busy in the house preparing bread when Araksi came to see me. Zenop had come also. On his way back he was arrested by the police. I put aside all my work and was going in haste to inform the Consul, but the gendarmes stopped me, and when I wanted to call on the doctor, they arrested me. Araksi also was arrested by the same gendarme who had arrested Professor Museghian, the teacher in the German School. Dr. Atkinson fortunately met Araksi and told the gendarme that she was one of his nurses in the hospital. A little later, two officers who had enjoyed her care in the hospital warned her, saying: "Mademoiselle Araksi, beware of going to the hospital; the Armenians in the hospital will all be wiped out." Finally she took refuge at Osman Effendi's, where Arsen and the orderly Peniamin were put up also.

Later we succeeded in sending news of our situation to Dr. Atkinson, and he promised to come and take us away at nightfall. An officer named Mehmed, who had been attended by Araksi in the hospital, tried to take Araksi to his house, telling her that Zenop and I had been rescued and were waiting there for her. Araksi did not fall into this trap, and Osman Effendi did not persist any further.

Afterwards she managed to get to Professor Luledjian's house, where she saw Miss Campbell. Arsen followed Mehmed Effendi, expecting to find me in his house. Dr. Atkinson and Miss Campbell took them to the hospital with two other officers. I was released at about nine o'clock by the personal intervention of the Consul, in whose house

I was accommodated for three days. All my children, except Araksi, were in the house of a Syriac. A few days later we were all near one another. The Consul succeeded in getting a written promise from the Government, saying: "Mrs. Mugerditchian and her six children will not be exiled at all."

A Turkish captain in the hospital, Khulusi Bey, becoming angry with Dr. Atkinson, sent a report to the Government saying that "he kept the family of the British Consul in his house." As a result he himself was expelled from the hospital.

We celebrated the New Year, 1915, in our house. Here Zenop and Araksi caught typhoid. Arsen was employed in a cigarette-paper factory, where he earned twenty piastres a day, but one day two of his fingertips were cut by the implement of an inexperienced man.

The Burning of the Prison

There were still some Armenian prisoners in the prison of Mezre awaiting trial before the courtmartial. They were Dr. Nishan Fermanian; Mr. Edward, the druggist; Mr. Yean; Dervartan, the pastor; and Unger Garo. The latter's body was pricked with needles, in order to get him to disclose some secrets. After the exile of the males and females the gendarmes called these prisoners out of the gaol, but they, knowing that they would be killed after unbearable tortures, refused to come out and declared that they preferred to die in the prison. The building was then set on fire and those who attempted to escape were shot.

The State of the Exiles

Mariam Simonian, our neighbour's daughter, of fourteen years of age, told the following story: – "They took us from Kharpout to Malatia, where they separated the males from the females, and transferred us to Frinjik, a village two days' walk from Malatia, where they undressed us all without exception. Some men in female clothing were discovered; these they killed before our eyes. Hagop, the young son of the Kaloyan family, was butchered like a sheep at his mother's knees; at tin.' same time they forced his mother to shout: *"Padishah tchok yasha"* ('Long live the Sultan').

"All the good-looking girls and young ladies were violated; even the girls of eleven or twelve years of age were tortured. Some women were hung from the trees and flayed. The same thing befell Busak Vartabed, the [American Evangelical] Bishop in Mezre. Numerous children were killed with bayonets. The family of Benneyan, the wife of Dr. Nigoghoss, the daughters of Tulgadentzi, and the family of Tenekedjian died of starvation in the desert. We were dragged for five months hither and thither and at last brought to Malatia, whence I escaped and came here."

Mrs. Paylun, the daughter-in-law of Fabrikatvrian, told the following tale: –

"On our arrival at Urfa we told everything that had happened to us. So the inhabitants of Urfa preferred death to exile. Miss Khanim Ketenjian, the daughter of the richest family and a graduate of the Euphrates College, joined the Armenian fighters and shot twenty to thirty Turkish gendarmes, and then she herself became a martyr. The Government could do nothing until they had the guns brought from Adana. So, at the command of German officers and artillerymen, the Armenians in Urfa were wiped out."

Mrs. Egsha Totovian described how they, a caravan of exiles composed of a thousand of the richer families, were placed in the khans, and then the men were separated from the women and were all killed. The women were panic-stricken and fled, leaving behind them all their belongings, ornaments, and valuables, in order to save their lives.

Once rumours were circulated that famine was prevailing in Russia. The reason, which was understood later, for this rumour was as follows. Shouts of: "Vrej, vrej!" (Armenian for "vengeance") were continually heard from the Russian Army. The Turkish Commander, not understanding the meaning of this, inquired of an Armenian artillery officer from Constantinople. "Sir," the latter replied, "the Russians ask for bread." So the Commander was very pleased, thinking that the Russians were suffering from a shortage of bread.

Another day rumours arose that the Pope had intervened on behalf of the Armenian Catholics, and that a pardon had been granted to the Roman Catholics. The same rumours went round about the Protestants, too, but those who came out of their hiding-places were taken outside the city and were killed.

Even if these rumours were true they were kept secret for eight or ten days, until the Armenians of all sects had been exterminated. Special overseers were appointed for those who were charged with the carrying out of the massacre. They waited for some time to make sure if the victims were all dead. The wounded in whom any sign of life was noticed were killed with spades, axes, knives, and bayonets.

On December 18th, 1915, Dr. Atkinson caught typhoid. Araksi attended him at nights. The doctor died within six days, on the night of the 23rd. Some of the Armenian artisans made a fine coffin of walnut for him. The Government sent a company of soldiers, and a carriage was to have been provided, but the Armenians refused it and bore the coffin on their shoulders.

The death of the doctor was a bad blow for the surviving Armenians; he was our last hope and refuge. Before his death he said to his wife in my presence: "I am sorrier for the Armenians than for you. I am glad to die, because this life is not worth living; but I was needed by these poor Armenians. Your future is safe."

Mrs. Mugerditchtan and the children

A Betrayal

An Armenian lady, N., who was supposed to be of middle but honourable class, and the sergeant were expelled from the hospital for their illicit conduct. The next day twelve young men working in the hospital were arrested for military service. The sergeant had betrayed them, and, owing to the desertion of six on the preceding night, it was a difficult task to save the remainder. The intention was to send them to the Labour Battalion. The major, having heard of the desertion of some, put the remainder under strict guard. Our Yervant was one of them. The sergeant in charge received strict orders to flog them, but the men made friends with him. When the major asked the sergeant if he was beating them, he replied that he was beating them to death and they could not move. He told the boys to lie down and moan as if they were ill.

There yet remained three days before Yervant was to leave. All my applications to the Commandant remained without result. I applied to the sergeant-major to allow Yervant to pass the night with us. He brought him at night and handed him over to us. We did not sleep all through that night. It seemed the last for us to be together.

I at once sent a letter to V. Effendi through an orphan, and asked him to come. We decided to apply personally to the Commandant, Muheddin Bey. It was long before midday when Araksi and I called on him. He received us politely and at our request he promised to release Yervant to work in the hospital in military uniform.

V. Effendi interceded for Yervant with the men in authority in the town, and at my request sent a letter to an important official.

The same night Yervant came home suddenly. Our joy was unbounded. A few days afterwards he put on military uniform and started his work. He was now quite free, whereas before he had not been able to leave the building. Two more were released with Yervant. These events must be regarded as nothing short of miracles.

Zenop in Dersim

As the arrest of Yervant was a good lesson to us, we hastened to send Zenop off to Dersim by the help of the Kurds, because Zenop was always taken from his appearance to be older than Yervant. Professor Kb. did his best for us in this matter, and bargained with an old woman to have Zenop taken safely to Dersim for £10.

We could not sleep until his first letter was received, which read as follows: –

"I have arrived here safely. I have made arrangements for you too with the Kurds, who will deliver my letter. Start at once."

But as Erzinjan had not yet been captured by the Russians, we did not dare to start. The American Consul also objected to our plan, saying that there was no fear for women, but nothing could be done for the boys above thirteen years and for those who had already been enrolled.

The Consul was probably right in saying so, as an *irade* was twice issued by the Sultan to put to the sword all male Armenians above the age of thirteen years, and the Executioners' Government of the Young Turks carried out the orders strictly, in accordance with a prearranged plan.

I had sufficient ground for fear. The German Consul had twice asked the Vali to have me imprisoned, from which, I understood from a reliable source, I was twice miraculously saved. He demanded my death, asserting that, if I remained alive and free, I would tell afterwards of all the atrocities I had witnessed.

There was no other means. With the fear of impending death before me, I decided to go to Dersim with all my children.

Our Flight to Dersim

Four thousand cavalry came from Constantinople. Sentries were put all along the Euphrates. There was absolutely no getting to Dersim. I sent this letter in cipher to Zenop: –

"Dear Zenop, – Let us know as soon as Erzinjan is captured by the Russians."

After some days passed in anxiety, I received suddenly a letter from Zenop informing me that the Kurds had opened a way to Dersim. The messengers told us that the Kurds who had come were famous Beys and could take us safely anywhere.

The same day Professor Kh. called on us and encouraged us in our audacious plan and said: "I would like to escape too, if my children were not so young." We had to sell all we had. Professor Kh. at once bought our things at high prices and paid in advance. Some of the surviving Armenians suggested the plan to us.

News had been received the day before that Erzinjan had been captured by the Russians and that the Turks had massacred all the Armenian artisans who were left there. We had only one reason for hesitation, and that was the insecurity of the passes.

I called on the Consul and asked for the money that I had

entrusted to him. He said I was going to endanger my life for the sake of my children. My reply was very simple: I told him that I lived for them alone. I entrusted a few things to him.

We prepared everything as soon as possible, and were ready to start at dark. A rendezvous was arranged where we gathered by ones or twos, and from there we started. We took a few small bundles and two Bibles. We were disguised to avoid recognition. When it was quite dark the three Kurdish Beys arrived at the rendezvous. We loaded on to the mules our luggage, which consisted of three little blankets and a little saddle-bag and our clothes. The Kurds gave us two mules and a horse, on which the luggage of four families was loaded, and the Reverend Bedro's sick wife rode on one of the animals. Yervant was obliged to carry some of the load on his shoulder.

We walked four or five hours without interruption. I became exhausted, and the Kurds, at the request of the children, gave me a horse. Yervant, Arscn and Araksi walked for thirteen hours through the night. Alice and Armine travelled partly on foot and partly on horseback. On the road to Dersim, as you know, there are many ascents and descents. We had to pass four hills in one night. No talking was allowed. At 10 a.m. we arrived at the groves of the village of Khozig, where, after taking breakfast, we slept for half an hour.

The Kurds woke us suddenly, saying that we were betrayed, and, trembling, we started again. We had taken off our boots and wrapped our feet in rags, but they were worn out before our arrival at Khozig. We began to walk barefoot through the stones and thorns. It should be mentioned that the Kurds were fully equipped, and that besides the three some others accompanied us now and then. The journey was exceedingly trying, but the hope of liberty and safety encouraged us all. Sometimes we encouraged each other with the hope of being in a free land, in Russia, very soon.

Yervant and Arsen carried Armine on their shoulders in turn, but neither the stones and thorns on the road nor our weariness could dishearten us. The Kurds cheered us, saying that we were three hours' walk from our destination, but it was the same refrain repeated throughout the journey. It would seem that the time of the Kurds is quite different from ours. After two nights and one and a half days we arrived safely at Dersim.

The Journey to Russia

We arrived at the bank of the Euphrates. The Turks had sunk all the barges, so we were obliged to cross the river by *apat*. The *apat* is a means of transport on the Euphrates made of three or four beams tied together. The Reverend Bedros lost his balance and might have been drowned if the Kurds, who are expert swimmers, had not saved him. There was no time to change his wet clothes. We were in a hurry to escape from the land of Sodom and Gomorrah, the land of ruin.

Having arrived at a village two hours away from the Euphrates, we hired fresh mules at very high rates. The inhabitants were very wild people and the village was a den of robbers. The people stared hard at us and were evidently looking for some opportunity of robbing us. Now we were all on mules except Yervant, who walked in order to help us now and then.

The Kurds treated us very kindly until we arrived at the bank of the Euphrates, but when we passed into the Kurdish land they became dictatorial to us. The young men played on the flute and some of us sang, and so we lightened the discomforts of the journey. And when "God the Indomitable" was sung, many refugees came out of their hiding-places and joined us, thus making up a numerous caravan, composed of twenty-five persons.

We felt ourselves free now, walking in a free land and breathing free air. A little time before we had all been too exhausted, not only to walk, but even to ride on the mules; but now we had forgotten all in breaking with songs and flute-playing the silence which terror had imposed on us for years.

One of the Kurdish Beys, on the pretext of relieving one of the mules, took some of the load and put it on his mule, for which service he charged us £10.

We passed the night on the side of a hill in the open air without beds, and after sleeping for three or three and a half hours, we started again at dawn. At 11 p.m. the Armenians of Dersim welcomed us like wedding- guests, at their village of Agtchunig. I must mention that we were entertained in the house of Kaimakam Jemil Effendi, your ex-messenger.

The Kurds in Agtchunig insisted on having all our things sold, saying that everything could be obtained in abundance in Erzinjan. We already had nothing left. The things kept in the bed covers were sold for £4. I had £6 in cash.

Then we started with five donkeys for the countryhouse of Idure, also called Ibrahim, who was to guide us to Erzinjan, but he had left three hours before our 'arrival. We were entertained by Mrs. Yazedjian of Tchemeshgadzak, who put her hut at our disposal.

Jafar, Idure's nineteen-year-old brother, when lifting up our sacks to guess the contents, took it into his head that there were thousands of pounds in them, and circulated false rumours that a family with thousands of pounds' worth of wealth had come. So, with several fools like himself, he fell upon us to rob us of our tilings, just when we were going to start with a fresh caravan of Armenians for Erzinjan.

Saidkhan, the son of Ibrahim Agha from Khodjushagi, robbed me of my gold watch. The same morning Zenop, with an Armenian boy called Luther, left for Erzinjan to inform Ibrahim Agha and Mr. Yazedjian what had happened to us.

Araksi and Arsen resolved to try and go in disguise to Beghavud to tell the Armenians and to have us rescued from this robbers' den. They were so skilfully disguised that I could not recognize them. They remained at Beghavud until I received a letter in the evening from Mr. Kaspar Boyadjian, one of the teachers in the Euphrates College, advising me to leave with Kasho, the Agha of Beghavud. I paid £4 10s. for a four hours' walk.

It was night when we started to go to Zogha. We passed the night in that village. The following day, at noon, we arrived at Ovadjik; having hired some mules there, we climbed up the Merjan Boghazi. It was impossible to move a step without a guide, even on the lower slopes of the mountain. It was a dangerous pass. The rivers, marshes, and rivulets followed each other. At last we arrived at Muzur, a rapid river, the bridge of which, consisting only of a beam, filled us with fear; but it was not the first time that the shadow of death had lain over us. It was 3 a.m. when we arrived at the foot of the hill and we had to climb it without rest.

Towards evening we met the Russian sentries, who welcomed us with joy. We had travelled for eighteen hours, so all were exhausted. It was the middle of August, and a cold, strong wind was blowing. We felt cold even in the corner where we had taken shelter. It was therefore deemed advisable to walk.

After three hours we arrived at the top of the mountain, which was 9,500 feet above the sea-level, and passed the night there. Here fifteen persons huddled up together to get warmth and sleep. We were fortunate enough to meet a Russo-Armenian, named Krikor, who made us wait until the dawn. He gave us his bed-cover.

In the morning he himself took us to a group of Russian soldiers, who were cooking, and entertained us with tea. The Russian sentries treated us so gently that we forgot for some time the terrors of Turkey. They supplied us with bread and sugar in abundance. It was here that our little Armine learned the first Russian phrase: "Dava'i stakan" (give me the teacup).

After having rested sufficiently, Mr. Krikor took us to a

vineyard where, for the first time for two years, we drank wine. At last, we arrived at Ekrek, a village four hours' walk south of Erzinjan, where we remained four or five days. Everything was plentiful.

Araksi, Yervant and Zenop went first on foot to Erzinjan, hired a carriage, and I followed them with the little ones. Fruit and vegetables were free in Ekrek, but nothing was left in Erzinjan. Alice and Armine fell sick. We were obliged to wait for one week.

There was no means of transport here. We had to travel on the waggons. We arrived at Mama- Khatun. Our driver and his friends introduced us to the officer in charge of the military transport, who kindly allowed us to be sent to Erzeroum by motor-car. He entertained us in his house for the night. His name is Yervant Zohrab. On the day following, at noon, we arrived at the historic city of Erzeroum. I must mention that two air-fights took place between the Turkish and Russian airmen in Erzinjan. The Turks were badly defeated.

It was Saturday when we arrived at Erzeroum, where Arsen caught typhoid. Three weeks after, as soon as Arsen had recovered, Zenop and Araksi fell ill of the same infectious disease. The weather was very cold, and we had no means of protecting ourselves. We were in a nearly naked condition. Seeing that all the children were in danger of being infected one by one, I deemed it advisable

57

to go with Yervant, Arsen, Alice, and Armine to Tiflis, where the weather would be comparatively mild, and where it would be very easy to communicate with you through the British and American Consuls.

Zenop and Araksi remained for forty days in Erzeroum, and after having recovered they came and joined us in Tiflis, just at the time when, by a happy coincidence, your telegram was received.

Here there are numerous Armenians, whose fate has been the same as ours and who want to go to America and are trying to get a pass. We intend to go to America or to Egypt, according to your advice. We are all in good health. Our liberty is nothing but a miracle, which we owe to God.

I send with this report my photograph and that of the whole family, from which you and Arpeny alone are absent, showing us in our Kurdish dress, and also in our present condition.

We are now anxiously waiting to see you, when I shall be able to tell you for hours and hours the details of the crimes which the Germans and the Turks committed in order to exterminate the Armenian nation.

One other thing I would like to mention before ending my report. The Turkish Government could never have carried out its diabolical plot to exterminate the Armenians if the

Armenian Committees had actually set on foot the plan of revolt which the Turkish Government expected. Neither would the Government have succeeded if it had not split up the young men by sending some to the Labour Battalion and exiling the others, so that nobody capable of bearing arms in self-defence was left.

At the beginning of the "exile" three Armenian tribes, one nomadic, the next half-nomadic and the third consisting of town-dwellers, took advantage of the friendship of their Kurdish neighbours and attempted to defend themselves; they are still holding out to-day. The majority are Armenians belonging to the Tayan, Soran, and Khaltan tribes. How fortunate we should have been if the Armenians had established friendly relations with the Kurds of our district! In that case, the calamity which befell the Armenians in Kharpout and Diarbekir would have been prevented or greatly mitigated.

The following episode may give you some idea of how heroically the Armenians in some places defended themselves. P., Q., V., T. and K. came to see me at Kharpout and asked me what to do in case the Turks committed in Diarbekir the same atrocities they had done in other places.

Without hesitation, I said: "There is no means but to defend yourselves or escape to Dersim." They did, in fact, defend themselves, and those alone were saved from the massacre who escaped to Dersim and took refuge among the Khian, Modgan, Khaltan, Botan and Milli tribes, according to a pre-arranged plan.

The general idea among the Turks is that a large part of the responsibility for the massacres and deportations falls on the Germans. Even the German missionaries played a great part, taking their arms from the poor people on oaths and by false promises.

It is true that the Armenians of Kharpout and Diarbekir were martyred and massacred in the most atrocious manner, and that their tomb is not known. But even as death came to them they had a smile on their lips, for they were steadfast in their faith in a new and Independent Armenia for their countrymen who survived.

Mb. Tovmas K. Mugerditchian

www.ingramcontent.com/pod-product-compliance
Lightning Source LLC
Chambersburg PA
CBHW021940040426
42448CB00008B/1162

9 7 8 1 6 4 4 3 9 1 0 4 4